I0826320

other titles by
Stewart S. Warren

~~~~~~~~~~~~~~~~~~

Shape of a Hill

The Weight of Dusk

Second Light

The Song of It:
A Travelogue of Norteño

Essence:
contemplations in image and word
with Corinna Stoeffl
~~~~~~~~~~~~~~~~~~

The Sea Always Near

The Sea Always Near

poems

Stewart S. Warren

The Sea Always Near

ISBN: 978-0-9827303-0-0
Publisher: Mercury HeartLink

Book design by Mercury HeartLink
Front Cover Painting: "Solstice" by Nancy Ortenstone, *www.Ortenstone.com*
Back Cover Photograph by Stewart Warren

Contents

——A Buzz Behind the Wheel

——Goodbye from Here

For the emissaries of love
who have commissioned this moment.
You know who you are
and you know what to do.

Up Country

You Called, Afternoon Rain

A steady farmer's rain falls, clouds
lower themselves and feel their way
through valleys, effortlessly enveloping
the hard terrain without demand,
without shout or hurrah.

White emissaries tiptoe across the top
of high conifer forests,
and like torn flags wave,
rise and become one
with the great whale passing overhead.

At the corner of the house a stock tank
catches runoff in two octaves.
Bobbing in the center
a piece of barn wood will become
a bird perch for morning bath.

In a city on the plains
you prepare your speech in a hotel.
We didn't talk about the weather;
you described people rushing on a street,
your roommate not yet arrived.

I've wasted enough time trying
to keep this desert grace to myself.
When the rain reaches Kansas City
wrap yourself in it—that's me
having travelled east all night.

ᘓ

Witnessing Whitney

the fire ceremony above Medanales

In the west, Cerro Pedernal
guides the sun through setting ripples
of orange, pink and purple.
Outside the blush of firelight

dogs bark at invisible rabbits where
witches pick flowers for the forgetful,
and the mesa turns, turns us
into the slender white arms of our galaxy.

You stand at the flames
articulating passages
for the homeward bound,
the way down into secret pastures

where ponies, even now,
wait for the watery moon,
the touch of your knees, the word
from your mighty heart.

Sparks cry and crack
with the passion of knowing—
these endless waves of heaven.
This bed of coals is your map,

your deck of telling cards, your cup
of divining tea. Each flame
is a different tongue.
You stumble before no one.

On this mesa you can ride
any language you choose.
Here, the faithful have ears;
the horses, vital velvet stories.

ca

Telling Time at the Alpine Alley Coffee Shop

I came the conventional way,
driving like rain, dodging coyote,
applied poetics under the wire.
I blurry-eyed down the street
sometime before seven, met up in the alley.

We broke smokes on the back steps,
too early for pedestrians,
we got ready to open taking turns
being back up, somebody's angel.

We sleep-walked the café, drove the kids to pizza,
small-talked the governor, catered the ruins.
Don't forget the potatoes—and the kindness.
In Mountainair we make 'em one at a time.

Everybody on the high here
is a transplant, artist of the month,
an evolved civilization unto themselves.
If you hang yourself out to dry
you'll be in Guadalupe County by noon,
married, divorced, forgiven,
the wind five times over.

At the front counter pilgrims have opinions;
in the kitchen degrees only count for cakes.
This is the Gran Quivera relocated,
the ghost-less side of town,
a mission of goodwill with optional hours.

I'm a frozen buffalo; I'm the sunrise
arriving by rail. I'm a square peg
and I'm raising this town
three feet off the ground. "Amen,"
said Mary, and pulled a pan
of hot scones from the oven.

☙

Astronomer's Night Off

This evening—clouds.

When I went to look for my friends
only a few shown through—
Venus, her fiery face
cool behind Earth's veil;
Sirius, dancing a tango
in a room where the butler
kept opening and closing the door;
and on the opposite shore, worlds
whose names I couldn't place,
shimmering off and on, unable
to articulate through the fog.

Tonight's deep space adventure then
will have to be the surface
of a water planet, a blanket
spread before the fire, star chart,
cup of chai, thoughts of you.

☙

City of Rocks

Venus rises, Mercury follows.
The Dipper has set, emptied,
risen again. I rise
like red iron to the surface;

have risen like the morning star
over soft pyramids of hills
and great swells of grasslands;
risen in the heart of wood burning,

through oak leaf starlet clusters,
sunlight speaking to rock.
In the first faint color of sky
coyote families crack into arias,

sing fallen rabbits back to heaven.
I'm at home here—prey and predator—
god godding into another
fire-edged, wild eyed day.

☙

Putting It to Music

Picking our way through outlaw poems,
the ones about holding the line and
tourists trying to pave the *pinto* patch,
we're thinking, maybe, a slow *bolero.*

The ones about holding the line and
it's no disgrace to be poor;
we're thinking, maybe, a slow bolero,
not a death chant but something mournful.

It's no disgrace to be poor,
watching stars fall and die on the mesa,
not a death chant but something mournful,
like shooting sparks from the welder.

Watching stars fall and die on the mesa
while I suppress the urge,
like shooting sparks from the welder,
to take the scalps of foreigners.

While I suppress the urge,
send a war cry to pierce the shadow,
to take the scalps of foreigners,
their dirty stacks of colonial bricks.

Send a war cry to pierce the shadow,
my teacher has put the pitchfork on the shelf,
their dirty stacks of colonial bricks,
there must be a better way to wake up.

My teacher has put the pitchfork on the shelf.
A *guapango* will fit with this next poem,
there must be a better way to wake up,
the grand sweep of Mesa Alta at twilight.

A *guapango* will fit with this next poem
coming down Forest Road 100,
the grand sweep of Mesa Alta at twilight,
two chain saws on top of the truck.

Coming down Forest Road 100,
the lights of Youngsville far below us,
two chain saws on top of the truck,
sopapillas y chile waiting in the kitchen.

The lights of Youngsville far below us;
God, get us down the mountain without a flat;
sopapillas y chile waiting in the kitchen and
thank you for another day in *Norteño.*

God, get us down the mountain without a flat,
tourists trying to pave the *pinto* patch,
y gracias por un otra dia en Norteño
picking our way through outlaw poems.

ꟹ

Up Country

I travel up country through flowering plum,
Globe Willow coming in, new water
starting its journey down.
I ask what makes this country
a refuge and a death chant,
because I used to live here

and have memories of Castilian dialect
running through family villages,
mud-heavy boots kicking a plank,
vendors on the roadside selling
punched tin and apples, saints
and dog tags swinging from mirrors.
I was a sinner here.

At first, you say, I'll just hide out,
but after while whatever was
the platform of your migration fades
in this rough-edged enchantment;
those boxes of water-damaged books
dying in the back of her shed, images
of the United States on barbershop
televisions no longer relevant.

The women I loved here were travellers, too.
They wedged gardens between
horse pastures and narrow seasons,
waved their shirts to keep the cows out,
redefined pioneer.

They saw me coming—hungry-eyed
and barely hitting the ground.
I split their wood, followed them into ancient canyons.
I couldn't see it up close, not then, I was
too busy wrestling my skin, outrunning ghosts.

If you didn't bring enough devils with you
the locals will loan you some—and all that time
you thought they were talking to themselves!

Those hillside slivers of *ejido* orchards, I swear,
are kept only by frost, wind, grace of rain.
If something falls on the ground up country
it's anybody's picking. By now you ought to know
what not to leave lying around.

I took a lot for granted here, but I remember
the sandstone touch of their hands
and the smooth moonlight swimming
in the curve above their hips.
But I'm not looking for old classmates,

so if it's all the same, you can remember me
going on down the road, howling just like I did;

and I'll remember angels with their wings
tucked under and their hair tied back,
turning that first shovelful of dark dirt,
letting new water in to flood the fields.

☙

Abiquiu, Moving On

If there's nothing you demand
you can soar the wild grasslands
all the way to Alberta,
know each trembling feather,
revel in humanity—
you can be the wind
embracing hearts without damage.

At the base of these trees
and along flowered curves
you hear a song in loving memory,
una memoria to everyone you once knew.
Every thought of love is written
in living rock, then dives
back into the core.

Looking up, you see veils of ice
strewn west by streams of wind,
a cross on every hill. Sierra Negra,
Black Mesa, Alma Obscura—
they named this table in dark cloth,
but you see light under baskets,
many herons returning.

You pruned the orchard hard this time,
survived the seasons of it,
burned the slash, didn't look back,
turned iron into petals. What now
will be your calling?

ᴓ

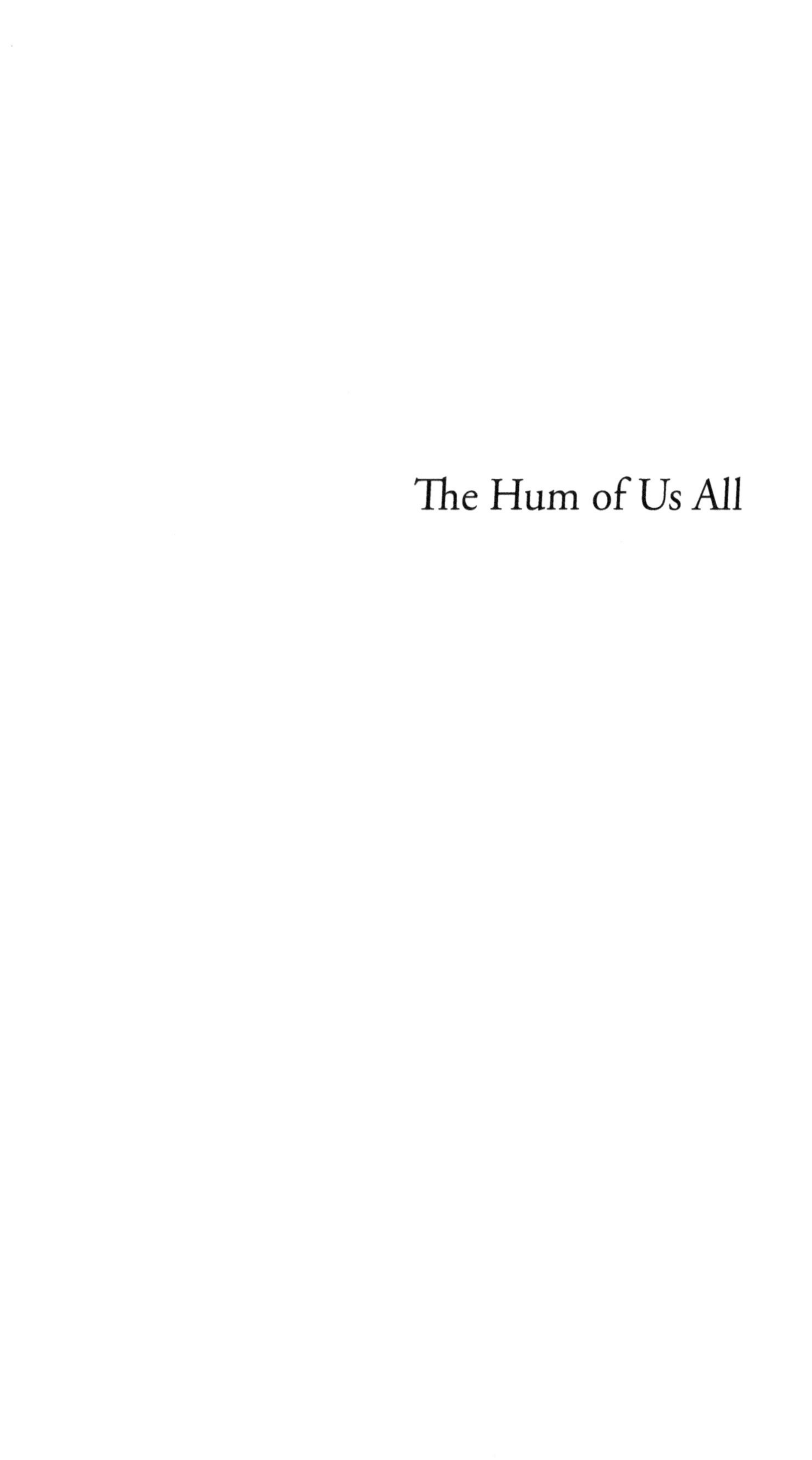

The Hum of Us All

Day Two, Metropolis

Driving nails so quietly
even my thoughts tip toe
as I unpack on the third floor,
my new apartment complex
five times larger
than the town I just left.
I write to the new owners—
treasure the silence, I say,

adore deep sky objects
visible with the naked eye,
the splitting maul you'll use
to loosen frozen firewood
from the bottom of the pile.
Treasure darkness.

A thousand refrigerators run
in one city block, street lamps,
porch lights, the artificial canopy,
the hum of us all.
Somebody opens up

the back barrels on San Mateo,
somebody coughs next door.

Soon, I'll let out my breath,
breathe this city as one and join
the hammering, the bleating,
the quickened pulse.

☙

The Doves

. . .fluffed for February, settled
midway into the White Ash

and without a coo preened themselves,
diving deep into piles of feathers,
closing the white outlines

of their eyelids with each plunge.
One, more pink than buff,
finished first and sat quietly

in the bobbing branches,
blinking contentedly in the tangle
of over-draping arms.

When they left I sat with my hands
folded, one resting on another,
long into the unruffled afternoon.

ﻬ

And Then, We Do What Comes Naturally

You have to imagine the crotch of a tree,
one leg meeting another in midair,
rough, uneven, offset; this,
the starting point of home.

She imagines—then so must you—
a basket loft, a bowl of twigs
lined with fine found objects.
Later, you see, they will arrive

warm and smooth, pecking for food,
thinking like beaks.
Or maybe there's no picture at all,
and one morning in the tree

where you first met she has settled
uninterested in things outside the niche—
even you, it seems.
For a while you sit near,

try to match the rhythm of her pulse,
talk to her about fields of grain
and warm evenings with just a stir.
Not interested.

Uneasy and still crazy for love
you start pacing on a branch,
tugging at flimsy twigs,
returning with sticks.

☙

Nakedness

The legs and arms of the sycamore
(beginning near the waist)
shed their flaky orange bark

and bare their nakedness, smooth
as snakes in water, shining
like a child stepped out of the bath.

The sun feels good, they say,
and though the sycamore is late to leaf
the same stirring of star stuff

writing itself upon this page, tunneling
through moldy hay and flitting
among juniper exploding red on the wind,

crouches like a cat
at the base of every bud.
Strands of spider wires glint in piercing light;

a bird sings from the top of my head;
the diamond of my mind
towers like a tree.

Good morning, we both say,
with no attempt to speak in unison—
though we do, anyway.

☙

Waking as a City

Albuquerque, Mid March

In the east an abrupt range,
a snow jagged silhouette,
the rock-cut vertical ruts of earth's wearing.
At the base a broom skirt of desert
slopes at an easy angle toward the big river.

Channels, dry or wet, sluice
across the tilted plain, some becoming
deep burnies, others disappearing.

And woven into those fingers and arms
of mountain runoff and pale orange sand,
a lattice work of wires and dwellings and highways
murmurs in the early hours of morning, becoming
an audible din as we rise from the earth
and flow out upon the land.

I open a door on the third floor
and let the city in—
the wakened hand of humanity.
I appear in a body. You appear as well.

Bud-laden trees, the very first
wasp of spring dizzying about the eve,
clouds being made on location—
such aliveness are we!

☙

Orchid

Your split tongue
turns back, beckons
with wispy ends

the speckled
butterfly poised
in the throat

of hope's escape.
Pale silver
moons float

on wide leaves;
they touch
but never collide.

ꕤ

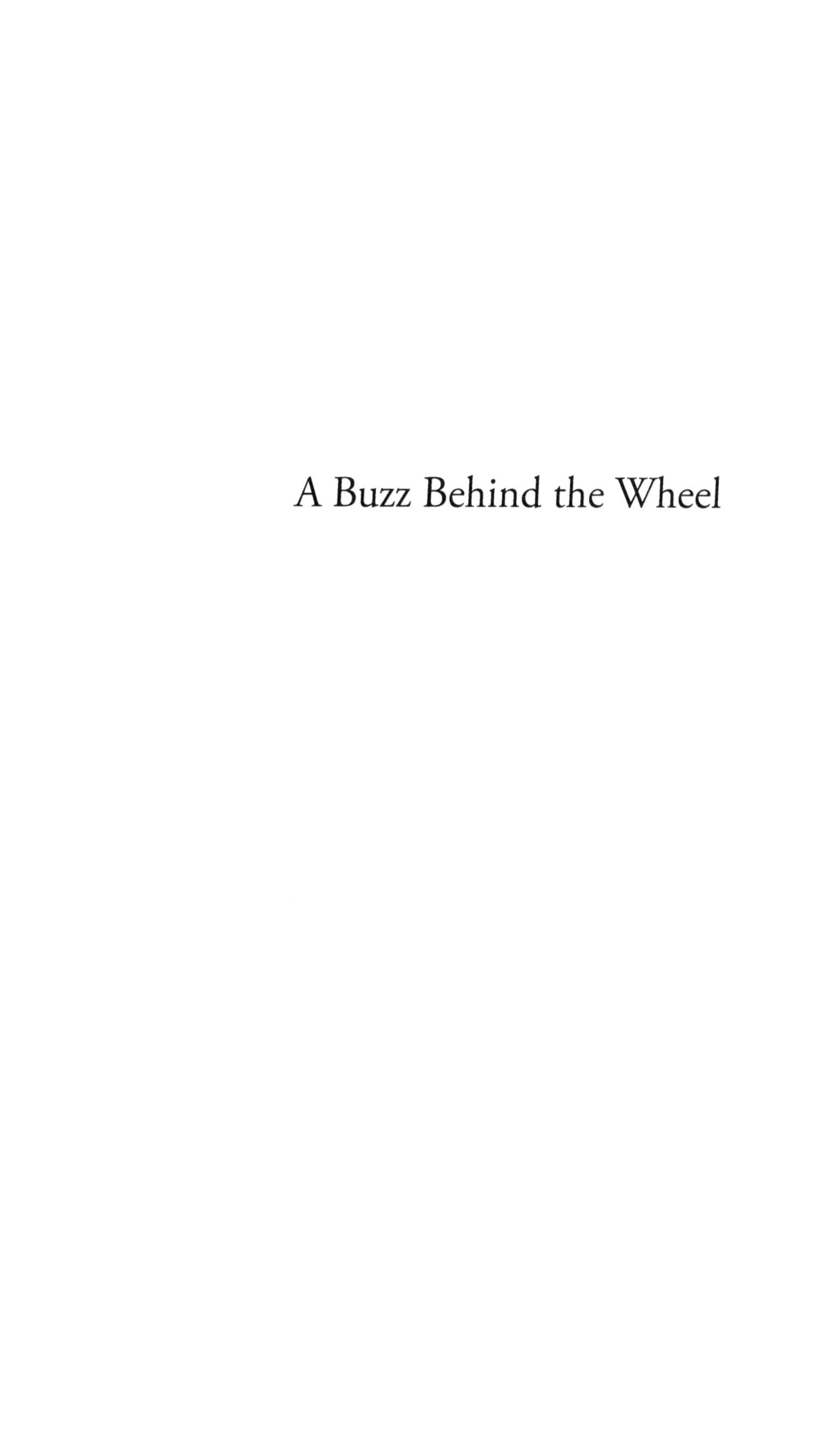

A Buzz Behind the Wheel

Correct Neurosis

To have a life in which
you're always on time,
in perfect step,

neither hero nor flunky,
in the middle or top third
of your class. A blue ribbon or two,
broken arm with everyone's name
signed to the cast, a movie
of flying graduation caps.

No jagged pieces on which
to get stuck, just that one
difficult year in school, then,
off to war, back again; business
as usual, Oh, maybe a little too much stress.

Quietly picking up the beat,
you're the metronome of community choir,
knowing when to come in,
when to resign, parallel parking
your forte, a spouse or two
through the life of the policy.

If you hadn't already lived that lifetime
you'd feel lacking right now,
which would be the correct neurosis
for someone always on time.

☙

Upright Man

Deep in red rock dinosaurs sleep in sheets
of pressed earth where oceans
rose, fell, sloshed then disappeared
beneath the shadow of time.
I walk now on the bones of all.

How I have judged my kind, our tools
of domination, our crouching,
our scramble to the top—
but I, too, am a fighter.

I fight for the music,
for the child's precious time with mud pies,
for the protected moment
in which the lily is allowed to open
and open and open.
I, too, am pushing, pushing
into the earth, mining memories
of molten and not-so-humble beginnings,
pushing for more
than the shallow stroke of mindless media.
I'm elbowing fear out of the way.

I am upright man and I'm covered

in the hot ash of warrior frenzy,
running before the flowing cup
of my own manufactured volcano,
holding on to my hat, throwing it
from suspension bridges.

I have murdered in the name
of one idea or another,
programmed captives, shot the hostages,
stood dripping over the carcasses of others.
And I have wanted so much
to be in love with you,
understood so little of these feelings,
these torrential spring tides, eclipses.

I dive with microscope and telescope
into the vast oceans of being
and it occurs to me that I am the instrument,
the crest of God's wave.

Of all the things that I have believed
to be true only a few prevail,
and this, for right or wrong,
is the expression I bring.

I have nothing to give, though I am given.

Star stuff is my fuel—I, my own witness,
and longing, in and of itself,
is the voice of the universe without words.

And though I cannot say where I go
or if I remain
these bones at my feet
and these worlds yet to come
have one constant blessing:
my seeing and my touch, and this
I call love.

ω

Time in These Streets

It was Monday
but it hadn't always been so.
It was that kind of millennium,
late to leave, lingering
on the corner; It was Monday
at the register and making change
was awkward, fumbling
with tokens, finding words
to reconstruct the world;
Monday on the streets, elbowing
our way down the line somewhere
important to be, a fantasy of appointment.

It was Tuesday and she was opposite me,
a signal fire between her eyes,
a shape inside a shape that I recognized,
lights coming and going, a buzz
behind the wheel.
It was a place we hadn't been, a time
unknown, a date in a borrowed car.
There was no fear of sharing thoughts here;
only thoughts that were real could appear.

It was the same rule but not the same sun;
waves—but not water—on a neighboring shore;
add-ons and plug-ins that resembled hands,
difficult things finally understood.
It was different moons and different blood;
seeing was the same, but extended.
Down in the street, Wednesday
had finally arrived.

☙

House of Rain

when your version of the world is done

You built cities on a hill,
taller and taller,
you became the elite,
called us commoners.

Your power is about how fast
you can pass a stone,
a shell necklace, electron.
Your worth is dependent

on trends, trade routes. Without water
you are a wisp on the wind.
Every crack of your whip ties you down
but we, my friend, are just passing through.

Your reservation lines
fade on paper, hold only bones.
We're not artifacts, objects
in a glossary of ancient terms.

We are the spiral journey,
a migration. Returning
to the inverted mountain
we follow the pearl words

of water dripping in a cave.
When your pipes and wires are dust
we'll be standing on the shore
of a great interior lake.

଼

Every Civilization a Shoreline

I hear the urgency of your voice
blown through the machinery
of your desire, the background roar,
rise and fall of industry and unrest.
I listen as your lover

between the hammer's ring and folds of press.
I wait for you on the center line
dancing up and down the fault,
rising in your throat a shout about to dream.
I follow you into the taillight night,
wait everywhere for your becoming.

On the shores of future deeds
I build signal fires, pour
the sand of time through my shell.
I am not without you.

Invisible by day I witness
the driftwood of your thoughts,
the pearls of your longing.
Your kindnesses leap
just beyond the reef in playful circles.
Nothing real you do goes unnoticed.

At night the sky is a seesaw;
in the morning mysterious tracks
wash out, disappear beneath rush hour.
Every moment leads to this one;
my breath goes back and forth with yours.
When you think of me
I am the onshore breeze.

ᘓ

To Reach Green Grass

The gazelles, in a tidal swell, migrate
north to south across parched Savannah,
snorting dust, tossing heads,
coming to the need of waving grass.
At the river's bank crocodiles
subdue their excitement beneath
slow eyes floating like blossoms.
The gazelles pile up, hooves digging
at the lip of momentum—
but the crossing must be made.

The crossing must be made,
the earth turn in its socket,
slender legs snap, blood
spill into the river. Sometimes
you leap to the other side; sometimes
you fall; sometimes it is you
who salivates through slacked jaw.
Afterwards, a small breeze passes
over calming waters, the waiting grass
at last, singing
between satisfying teeth.

☙

The Scene at Taiji

After the Japanese fishermen
drive the leaping dolphins
into the cove by beating
on metal rods held in the water,
and their high horsepower engines
jerk and churn and whine
as babies are separated from parents,
and the friskiest *Flippers* are auctioned
to sea aquariums for pleasure models,
the fishermen drink and congratulate and leave
hundreds of captives overnight
to click and cry in shallow waters.

And the next morning
after they make a beach fire
and warm their hollow hands
and tell stories of conquest
(whales from horizon to horizon),
they step into their boats
with their gaffs, their harpoons,
their imperial pride, and render
this high-walled ancient cove
with its leaves fluttering like Buddhists prayers
and its gentle crush of turquoise waves

a torrent of blood and frantic slapping.

And after the gasping bodies
are hauled into boats
and taken away as meat for market
and the cove is crimson and still
and a bucket of red seawater
is thrown on the smoldering coals,
the Japanese fishermen light cigarettes
and take the numbing smoke deep
into their gray lungs.

☙

To Flood the Fields

In the backbone of the Three Gorges Dam
34 million cubic yards of cement
continue to cure while mammoth lock doors
creak slowly open and closed
and pleasure ships and generators turn
under the apprehension of cloud burst.

The 660 kilometer dragon filled its belly
with waters of the mighty Yangtze
and thirty thousand years of human culture
let go its last breath beneath rising tears.
From eleven hundred small villages
and thirteen modern cities
over a million people were displaced, evacuated—
China on the move like a moon.

Residents of the underwater cities
were paid by the brick to demolish
their own factories, office buildings,
homes. Swinging sledge hammers,
wheeling carts, toting woven baskets,
they leveled neighborhoods, buried
the smells of rice and fish and vegetables,
of incense and sex, of sharpened pencils,

high tea and cut flowers; buried
the words of someone saying,
"Good morning, old master,"
to a grandfather repairing a chair, the yip
of a dog following children to school, the chatter
of friends hanging laundry on the porch—
all buried in a tide of dust, now submerged.

When the last gates were closed
and the waters rose over smashed temples
and forgotten cloth dolls, scientists
recorded a wobble in the earth resulting
from the slosh of mountains, but
who heard the cry
of cranes looking for their nests?

ಬ

To a Young Poet

While being taught to think, you're sharp;
some blade slipping from your sleeve
ready to cut other tongues. Forget
that row of chaired examiners, engineers;

they can only take you in squares
that end in a corner of their room.
Have your discernments, but first the juice
from your melon heart. Leave dissection

to med students, talk show hosts.
Love as much as is allowed
this moist flicker of a world.
It's yours—for now—every blue turn.

There is a day on the edge of town
where the corn is burnt
from too much looking. You'll have to
eat that meal, too, so water

whatever you pass. These moments
go from hand to hand—keep moving.

ଓଃ

Goodbye from Here

A Wounded Horse Approaches

A wounded horse approaches,
limp leg held above the ground.
It's not as heavy as you think, lifting her
to your breast, holding her
warm solid body neck to neck.

Someone else will say you were alone,
struggling. Someone else
will cry at the end of the story.
But grace has turned every corner,
some happiness shaped itself
with every breath. Circumstance
is concrete, corruptible, so brief.
The whiteness of the page
goes on forever.

Look again. Wasn't I there
in the glint of growing grass;
the empty stolid silo;
the dull cold strike of the plow;
the morning road out of town? There,
in the puppy-like efforts and growling of others;
our clumsy good byes.

Arriving,
you say to yourself, I'm sorry,
I didn't understand, please,
by all means, continue.

Now that you've heard the music,
taken the liniment,
I'll be with you on the inside
chiseling imaginary bricks, unraveling
the thread at the middle, following
the scent of fresh-cut hay—
your horse waiting in the meadow.

☙

Dropping My Folks Off After School

I took my parents to their homeland,
each to the town of their birth,
my father to Chelsea, mother to Sapulpa,
both towns on "The Mother Road," Route 66,
but that highway was born in '27,
long after my parents had arrived.

I didn't take them there
at two o'clock in the morning
when we could have slipped in and out unnoticed.
I didn't take them on a Wednesday night
during canasta or bible study.
I didn't take them in their coffins
or those dark red plastic boxes.

Where shall I drop you off, I asked,
driving up and down curbless streets,
clumps of daffodils standing beside rock,
metal siding from the '60s,
ten foot wide satellite dishes, patina of moss.
I wasn't in a hurry— this was their day.

Look, I said to my dad in Chelsea,
the old brick auditorium is a Family Dollar!,

and I considered his years in office,
what social discourse, community
and public speaking might have meant,
now the gaudy yellow rectangle
of consumerism bolted to its face.
Here, dad? . . . just kidding.

Or maybe near the cistern where
the butter was kept in a stone chamber,
spring water gurgling underneath—
just a little north of that tree, must have been.
Was that your rope swing?

Back on "The Main Street of America"
a pickup passed hauling a boat twice its size,
twin MerCruiser Inboards, TV in the cabin.
So long, dad, I said.   Where to, mom?

In Sapulpa the trees run north and south,
the presidents east and west.
She might have lived near Maple and McKinley
but she didn't say. It was Monday
and the waitress kept making mistakes,
asking for forgiveness, losing focus.
Underneath the chaos
of her own troubled thoughts
and trying to please her boss

innocence was the order she placed.
I tipped my hat, then left
without getting a meal. After all,
it wasn't my day to take care of her—
and yes, I forgive you—
as I turned the corner
she returned to the kitchen
with the new girl she was training.

Beneath the asphalt of Main Street
red bricks crumble unnoticed,
all the big trucks now humping the Interstate.
On my way out I stopped to watch
the Union Pacific at Hickory Street
pulling seven new tankers, no caboose.

ର

Portals of Sleep

The house trailers and lofts
that I did not call home
played out quickly like cards,
throw away hands.
But even to those porches,
spare rooms and vacant lots
with tall grass trampled to make a bed,
I turned in the morning
and thanked the earth.

On a high mountain pass
east of the Fraser River
I broke into a gas station one night
and balled up on the tile floor
to escape the vagaries
of a howling Canadian winter, then
that abandoned school bus
southwest of Cuernavaca
where Eduardo kept one eye
open for the Federales.

It's not just rest I needed,
the rejuvenation of cells
and heavy black cloth of sleep

pulled over my senses,
but all that catching up to do,

those errands, reports, and of course,
the well at the center of town,
and my other family
passing in and out of night's house.

☙

The Whereabouts of Carol

Oklahoma, I'm going to talk about you now,
but I'll leave your family
out of this. The Osage Hills I guess
were something
of legend, draw knives, crude oil,
Ponca Indians, and for me a stretch
of blacktop north through green bottom land,
stony curves to the top—
to Bartlesville. We took a pineapple

to a Friends Meeting where silence
raised up earnest speakers
like random kernels of popping corn.
Our long hair didn't scare those farmers,
the fruit received like a prodigal son.
When I turn back I see now
the whole meeting house was a plantation.

So I'll just come right out and say it:
Carol from Bartlesville.
If there's any time I wish I'd been awake. . .

I still dream cotton curtains blowing
in an open window, tending early garden.

Good soil up there if you stay west
of the flint rock, but I brought her down
to Tulsa, yelled at her
for leaving the iron on.
And you think I'm stupid now?

My first stomp dance was up that way
but I never let it count.
It felt good to shuffle in the dirt
but I was too young to wonder
what happened to lost feathers.
Later I wanted to return
to every place I'd ever been
with my own car, walking papers,
a keen eye making sharp rights
down whatever road
said it might know a patch of dark soil
and the whereabouts of Carol.

☙

The Story of Me

The story of me is overgrown,
a southern town with squirrels
leaping through alleys, Creeping Virginia
and Wisteria, doves and trash trucks
starting the morning, pots of beans
simmering on stoves, few emergencies
until the drunks wake up.

The story of me was going to *be somebody*,
reciting foreign alphabets, painting presidents,
rehearsing for talk shows, branding that link,
putting my napkin in my lap.
The story of me has never fixed anything.

The story of me swings from one narrow window
to another, sees birds flying backwards,
thinks it must be so. The story of me
waits at a station, luggage piled high
on a dolly, porters running up and down
looking for the bride.
The story of me can't come any closer.

The story of me shoots movies on location,
prison camps, bedrooms and truck stops,

all this rising from Oklahoma red dirt
but still not a lick of shade, or sense.
In fadded photos Field Hollers keep time
with hurt and hope, the sharp husks
and tender shoots of cotton plants.
The story of me hears rifles cocking,
puts its head to the ground.

The story of me wanders to the edge of town,
scrambles through sumac and oak,
finds a bare spot on top of the hill, reaches
into the sky but can't feel itself, shivers
when the sun goes down, suspects
there may be someone else nearby.

The story of me steps outside, looks down,
discovers an origami unicorn on the doorstep,
begins to wonder about origin and longevity.
The story of me is a legend
in its own mind.

☙

Goodbye from Here

Ground fog in waves hugging farmland,
scattered trees coming and going in the mist.

An occasional break reveals low rolling hills,
the place of my birth, crimes under the blood,
a stand of deer, my ancestors.
A voice without sound, a thought without words
is someone saying, There's nothing left to do.
A spiral of yellow-green light snaps into place.
I've been a traveller on that convict's road.
You know the one.

At times my feet barely touched the ground but my heart,
my heart loves this land and all that rises from it.
I admit being in a hurry, as hesitant
as I am eager for that Taboric Light.
Deep down or higher up I believe we're all deserving—
otherwise it just doesn't make sense.
But what now, with no task left for my design?

Bull dozers and earth movers shake the stage,
claw her skin in huge gaping swipes.
You're a tragic classroom, and I, still so young.
Leave it alone, they say, you're done.

Then should I go to each clump of grass,
every beige bird and to the house
of every stranger that took me in—
or will I say goodbye from here,
touch everyone at once?

I see those rolling hills and damp oaks in the distance
and my body reaches out to run
with those meandering rivers of boyhood, of lifetimes.
Cimarron, North Canadian, Arkansas, Verdigris,
your blood is in my veins, your long-legged water birds
swoop across this dream.

But I can't say I'll miss you,
missing is something we made up.
And I still don't know what it is that I've done,
but, according to them, it is enough.

ଔ

Red Desert Dust

with appreciation for Li-Young Lee

As they take her away (again)
I hear my mother wailing,
wilting for policemen, male authorities,
her torn nightie catching
on the ambulance and groomed grass
of austere Southern gentility.

This is the drunk mother I want
to never come back. Die.

The love of this mother plucked like a parrot
at the mirror she tried to make of me,
fussing, always fussing with fear.

I am not strong enough, I said
without moving my mouth,
to keep raising her from the dead,
to hope and hope and hope.

When my older brother raised a kitchen knife
to my mother's throat I spoke up,
disarmed him with water.

But when he insisted I meet his *new friend*
with a pipe and pinch of weed
I followed his words on a string.
I went limp. I went to the penitentiary.

I hear my brother's love pacing
back and forth on a slippery plank,
waiting to be received—forgiven.
But the love of the prison guards lays locked
in a cell for which only they have the key.

My father refused to stay and watch
his first son's casket lowered into the grave
so I left the cemetery with him.

Might as well—take care of the living.
"Father," I called him, shaking his hand
and only later did I venture "Dad."

The love of my father shone
in the ways he held back, his refusal
to raise a soldier like himself.
We both had the ocean and the eye of the artist,
but I have been the one to give it voice.

Later, he disowned me—
or pretended to for the rest of his life.

You can only save yourself, they said.
But what self do they speak of:
the made-up idea of me or the truth
I know but can't prove in the streets?

Nevertheless, I've got my own box of history
to burn in the fire of remembrance, some of it
washed up from ship wrecks long ago and far away.
I don't even recognize some of this stuff.

The love of God is a tree I fall early each spring
because I think it must be dead.

But the arm that swings the axe is also
the root that sprouts again. It's a no fault deal.

Later, in a silence which can only point
to that place that cannot begin
and cannot cease from becoming
I saw the small moments of their hands fumbling
with this same heart latch.

Undone, I let their love wash in,
stand with me, fill the night sky.
Mother, Father, Brother, I cried.

The love of my friends holds me kindly;
they suspect the tempest of this storm, fragile string.
If ever I pulled back, it was only a duty
of the highway, a knee jerk reaction.

True, our joining may be the only thing
that matters, but still,
the high plains remain my home.

The love of red desert dust
is my witness in the world.
It covers me, then,
I let it fall through my hands.

☙

Whose Only Purpose Is Love

Yesterday I sent angels into the world.
I sent them to wait in unpretentious places,
concealed in grandmother scarves
carried by children fleeing the black trains,
to that hiding place beneath the pounding table,

to the fields where women tend crops
while giving birth with the other hand,
to corners of overgrown lots
where toads and bugs speak in tongues.

I sent the angels ahead
to perch patiently behind your teapot,
in the slender voice of your favorite pen;
I sent them, these angels
who already know your name.

You knew to look in the grand fall
of water in mighty canyons,
the hug of the moon (steady companion),
the tiptoe of songbirds across the morning.

Now you look in the small places, any edge
where light meets shadow, the open field

of suspended judgment, the pulse
of your hand in time—angels everywhere,
the angels you sent.

☙

The Sea Always Near

From the desert I hear the ocean,
the rolling surf, variation of breakers,
and further out something like a city,
a roar of sorts, a universe sparkling
mysterious on each surface.

I hear gulls announcing their arrival
driven onshore like arrows, crying
in the mist, tumbling for fish.
And from the chalky cliffs
I hear my mother's steady song,

unquavering now
beyond the pardon of death.

She cries, too; cries
to gather her two sons to her—
one ripped from the shore of day, the other
preparing for the depths of night.
And her two husbands, clean
and strong now, having also finished
their days of fishing.

God, how my heart swells
at the smell of seaweed, the song of rock,
feel of tar between my toes, salt
and sand drying on my face.

And how I yearn for the pull
of the night tide, at sunset
the wind changing direction.

ꕥ ꕥ ꕥ

www.ingramcontent.com/pod-product-compliance
Lightning Source LLC
LaVergne TN
LVHW020652100826
845148LV00012B/2455

* 9 7 8 0 9 8 2 7 3 0 3 0 0 *